Four Dispositions of War

FOUR DISPOSITIONS
OF WAR
M. J. MOBLEY

THE **BLACK SPRING**
PRESS GROUP

First published in 2022
Maida Vale Publishing, an imprint of The Black Spring Press Group
Grantully Road, Maida Vale, London w9
United Kingdom

Typesetting User Design, Illustration and Typesetting, UK
Cover art Juan Padron
Cover photo M. J. Mobley, taken with his camera in Afghanistan, theatre of war, 2012.

The publisher has followed American spelling and grammar at the request of the poet

ISBN-13 978-1-913606-22-0

CONTENTS

... and in the stone a new name written, which no man
knoweth saving he that receiveth it.
   —*Revelation 2:17*

That I may rise, and stand; o'erthrow me; and bend
Your force to break, blow, burn, and make me new.
   —John Donne, from 'Holy Sonnet 14'

PROLOGUE

It is the purpose of this poetry collection to serve as a field manual for those seeking ways to understand the myriad complexities that surround the military industrial complex and the creation of the modern soldier; except in those cases when the understanding of the military industrial complex and the creation of the modern soldier is exceedingly simple.

It is the purpose of this poetry collection to bridge the gap between those both intimately familiar with military service and those who have no connection to military service whatsoever; except when the work attempts to further drive a wedge between these two divergent parties.

It is the purpose of this poetry collection to make clear that the creation of every soldier begins in youth. Every action, event, and moment acts as a mold in which, with proper care and further training, a competent and capable soldier might emerge over a lifetime; except in those cases in which the creation of a soldier takes place suddenly and violently.

It is the purpose of this poetry collection to ensure the reader does not mistake kindness for weakness; except when weakness will best serve the greater good and a facade of superficial kindness can best be used to inflict even greater damage.

It is the purpose of this poetry collection to make clear that all people, characters, events, and incidents portrayed in this work are fictions of conceit. No identification with actual persons (living or deceased), places, buildings, and products is intended or should be inferred; except for those people, characters, events, and incidents that are very real.

It is the purpose of this poetry collection to make clear that the only real experience one can have is that of war; except where otherwise noted.

CHAPTER 1: FORMATION

First I was made by thee, for thee...
   —John Donne, 'Holy Sonnet 2'

THE WAKE-UP CALL YOU NEED

Commissioned to breed you,
Break you, to unify the empire,
The clay footed magistrate.

I am.

Poet, scholar, warrior,
Descended—out of, by—*Caput Mundi*,
Fathered through, for, Caligula.

I am.

Anti-Alpha, Anti-Omega,
The *logos* of a new world,
Spun in centrifugal imaging.

I am.

Flat bellied, barrel chested,
Rippling, sinuous tiger meat,
Wrapped round a titanium frame.

I am.

Pulling back fresh curtains of fear
To reveal true intentions,
Naked as Achilles' heel.

I am.

A song to the gods
Of our civilized traditions
Casting your nature aside.

I am.

The names of ancient fathers
Slain in domination
Saying *to hell with all* in malice.

I am.

Deep within the purpling liver, putrid
Spleen of all those we failed to conquer
So that you might turn, forge, learn anew.

That I am.

Revolution found in the deep swallowing
Of harsh truth. From dust to dust,
Providing new skills for original sin.

A PROPER IMPERIAL CHRISTENING BY WHICH YOU MAY JUDGE YOUR OWN NATIVITY

Launch over the side of your crib and land feet first onto the braided rug serving to silence first steps toward sacrificial infant combat, a vision projected in the obsessive profession of future urges, a pampered escape to the room where women come and go, talking of life's littlest innuendos.

Talcum, singed hair, the hint of cat's breath mingle in the thick air of conquered dreams.

Be cradled.
Be wrapped in swaddling clothes.
Be rocked to sleep under the soothing sounds
    of mid-century ovum drying the matted lanugo still clinging
    to innocence.

This is your foundation.

The watchful eye of a dystopian future arrives and knows precisely how lots are cast.

Glide then through straight and narrow streets returning to an infant home and preach in the temples of your youth. Let the good news reflect these infantile movements across a wet lawn, your heavily soiled diaper bearing burdens, blurred memories of soft, capable hands, the ever-dimming light in the distance the sole reminder of the home you have left.

THAT EARLY TRANSFORMATION
YOU MUST ENDURE

A butterfly is a peculiar soldier.

But let us now discuss what it might be like to wet our trousers in
elementary school, marinating in pungent thoughts, refusing to go
outside for recess until the capable instructor, an experienced veteran
of classroom dynamics who smells of moth balls, red carpet, and
church hymnals, reaches into a magical storage closet to produce
the most dazzling pair of plaid bell bottoms you have ever seen.

Now flourish. Flutter away to join resentful peers engaged in games
of jump rope and kick ball, friends who will shout *those are not the*
trousers you were wearing earlier.

But we must face the music: these are the trousers we were meant to
wear. These are the trousers that will announce our entrance into a
new kingdom. These are the trousers in which we might bring in the
sheaves, pledge allegiance to the flag, and one day, fly off to distant
and exotic lands.

ASIDE ON CAIN AND ABEL AND THE EFFICACY OF PROPER SACRIFICE

Those are my best days when I shake with fear
    That my sacrifice failed to please a past
Full of starts and fits in which no one asked
What interest was given on well-meaning years.
What flag-draped savior emerged in my heart
    Bursting forth in power and glory
    With the promise of the story
Revered by the state and the soldier's mark?
Then we few, we thoughtful plodders, seeking days
    In a banished future conquering none,
    Touched by a land dragging boys along
By vestments of freedom and the civilized way
    Of killing in the name of liberty,
    Banished to the Nod now safe here in me.

INSTRUCTIONS FOR PARENTS WHO WISH TO RAISE UP A CHILD IN THE WAY THAT HE SHOULD GO WITH FOLLOW-ON INSTRUCTIONS FOR ALL NEW RECRUITS

Fathers, take your sons
To McDonald's for breakfast
In celebration of the childlike exuberance
Found in games of youth football;
Raucous affairs these
Balls tilt, lift, and bounce
Through complicit hands and fervent feet
In reverberations felt across conquered wildness.

Mothers, stand as young men attempt
To pass a rocket through the eye of another
In the promise of civilization's play-land
Maintaining your son's honest sportsmanship;
That elusive code
In which the player kneels and shakes
Off the guilt of their power
In waves of code burning repressed natures.

Sons, on these festive mornings
Order the biggest breakfast from your clown-shoed idol.
Throw your entire heart into the celebration.
Pour syrup on your pancakes,
    syrup on your eggs,
    syrup on your sausage patty,
    sweeten the salvation found
    on this thin paper plate,

Do this in stark contrast to your father's
Strong, black coffee and cheap aftershave
So that you might stave off the creeping melancholy
Found in your newly discovered spirit of contempt.

THE BREAKFAST OF SUPERSTARS

You will never be given over
        To Honey Nut Cheerios,
        Froot Loops,
        Or Cap'n Crunch.

You will receive your manna
        By way of Golden Tastee-os
        Fruit Rounds-Ups,
        Commodore Crispies

Delivered in unwieldy cellophane bags
        Ripping, splitting wide
        As you search
        For the elusive toy.

The others will find their luck
        In magical Lucky Charms.
        While you get nothing
        But un-Fortunate Talismans.

But they will taste so sweet
        When you eat them off the floor,
        Having spilled the contents
        Of your giant sack
        Across the boiling sea
        And onto the backs

Of those affluent Trix eaters who
Hate and despise our Illusions.

THOUGHTS ON ARTEMISIA I OF CARIA

QUEEN OF THE GREEK CITY-STATE HALICARNASSUS AND ALLY OF XERXES

When she is embraced and open to most men,
    A nagging thought becomes too real:
    That any man might embrace with zeal
A desire to fight, to make amends
To the three-personed soul found hidden
    Under feminine folds of flesh that greet
    A new land's fate, the fantastic feat
Of sensing just a whiff of her affections.
Impetuous men think it nothing to shed
    Masculine guilt, don the soft armor
    To take on the wild beast within woman's
Holiness, her bifurcated law spread
    Across mad seas, directing uncertainty
    And dying in her mythic battle pleas.

YOUR EXPOSURE TO THE SOLDIER'S DILEMMA

In a distant time, in a distant place, a woman gives birth to a boy.
The boy is healthy, strong, in control. As he grows, the young boy,
imprisoned in the naivety and idealism born out of his forefather's
past, knows only one truth:

Heaven and earth are his for the taking.
And yet…

Hindered by circumstances of ignorance.
Unaware of realities present in cartography.
No escape from the smothering mediocrity of his surroundings.
And so…

He sets out as one does in those days and plants his healthy, intelligent
seed into those who will accept him, follows his mythologies and,
with disciples in tow, wanders out of the land of exile in search of
the all-knowing.

In his sojourn the young man finds himself in harm's way, a warrior
called upon to defend his honor. Small, white trucks filled with
silhouettes, filled with mummies, filled with lies and deceit, creep
past his secured position in village after village in hopes of escaping
their own geographies, in hopes of sowing their seed in all who will
accept them, hunters and gatherers in search of their own lands,
seeking to stitch up an invasive wound.

This young man, in a distant place, in a distant time, has his men
take up positions along adobe walls and mud huts paralleling village
arteries as the slow-moving platelets slide into view, a parade of

sleeping pills swallowed with a silent reserve, slipping down the alley seeking a place to dissipate and renew.

And yet…

Shots fired.

Without hesitation, this strapping, healthy, intelligent young man maneuvers towards the conflict and begins directing withering volleys of fire upon the truck's occupants. All thirty-four members of his element, all thirty-four glorious heroes of the day become fixated on this one means of escape and relief. All thirty-four men commence to bring the entirety of their collective firepower to bear on the silhouette's essence emptying the conveyance of its untried contents.

And so…
He is renewed.

PREPARE TO MEET BANDITS ALONG THE WAY

On a youth group hunting trip
Reverend will say:
A raccoon's penis is always hard.
Here lies one before us even now.

Slick pink baculum rises
Like an octopus tentacle taxidermied
In the salty brine of confession.
Does yours ever get like that?

Pentecostal fire flickers
Across babbling tongues.
The light shines dim
On the prophet's thin lips revealing

This fearless dictator's priapic intent.
Eyebrows rise in unity of confusion
As our king skins the lifeless corpse
To look exactly like us.

TRUTH FOUND IN THE SIEGE
OF THE SOGDIAN ROCK

Lest the world flesh, yea, devil put thee out
    And place climbers upon high places that insist
    Give up this doomed boulder. Live life in us.
Hold on to nothing when you hear them shout
Allegiance to the simpler tools of the heart.
    A warring love knows only tattered truth.
    Conquerors come in waves. No lie can soothe
The thought of your once impenetrable fort.
Thrusting arrogance to a hidden ideal
    Results in a growing timeline of mistakes.
    So they climb on in a *me* revolution,
Clinging through the night to uplifting faith,
In search of obedience found in order,
Fighting as both zealot and martyr.

PREPARE NOW FOR YOUR OWN PERSONAL D-DAY

I stole my father's shoes and wore them to school,
Weathered wing tips creased at the toes
Where bones stretch ruthless and free.
Thick, woolen tube socks spark passion
In the frictions of newfound self-reliance.
I flop to the front of the class reciting
Matthieu aime son pays plus que… comment dit?

I stole a condom from my father's dresser,
Kept the tool in my front pocket,
A weapon superfluous to future conquests.
The all-natural, long-lasting, work-a-day rhythms
Of beachy invasions unleash vain glories,
Rip through the choking mask of machine gun haze,
The promises of arrival when we are finally whole.

In a father's oversized shoes
There is no need for the sheathed speed bump
Protection of your own self-centeredness.
Combat patience is a slow slog through a slippery slope
Of landmines and improvisations.
With proper preparation we might one day outgrow
These phallic training wheels, latex swim rings,
The fear of the unknown,
Like a new recruit learning a trade.

YOU MUST EMBRACE YOUR INNER LIAR
IF YOU ARE TO UNDERSTAND ANYTHING

To win a coveted blue ribbon in the county fair
Simply copy—word for word—a poem about a horse
That is getting old and needs to be put down.

Judges lap those stories up.

You must learn to take credit for your destiny,
Stealing words that never put up a fight,
Conquering carnivals in the name of efficiency.

You have learned to fashion progress
From the material emotions of others,
So that on the day,

Judges will be eating out of your hand.

Once they realize the horse in your bad poetry
Once ran free inside a mother's magazine
Sitting next to the toilet in a dilapidated home,
Where soldiers are not born,
But are forged out of necessity,

The damage will have already been done.

CHARLEMAGNE'S SAXON WAR AND YOU, A VIGNETTE

Thy true grief, for he put it in my breast,
    As well, ensuring a conquering for gain,
    Pretending to know the gravity of pain,
As he hands the yoke of service to this mess.
No more will anything be called divine,
    Weighed down by prophetic force foretold,
    Baptized by fire while promised streets of gold,
We know the shame, know the stealing of time.
Following twists and turns, the fall of free souls,
    We march. Onward someone's soldiers
    Finding our empire mediocre
Once respecting the only kings who fought
    We now stand as eager fools waiting our turn,
To kiss the rings of war hawks too scared to serve.

AN ITEM ON A TO-DO LIST WE ARE GUARANTEED TO NEVER COMPLETE

Build a canoe with calloused hands,
Rough-hewn, stripped bare,
Not necessarily sea-worthy,
But maybe just good enough

For a lake, or a pond,
Capable of navigating small streams,
While carrying boyhood dreams
Violently caught in a swirling,

Over-crowded ditch, the tiny leafing
Of youth now watched via probing eyes,
As our vessel picks a path
Through rivulets after a hard rain.

HASTINGS AND PATIENCE

Of thee and thy house, which doth in eating heal
    The wounds of a two-front attack that burn
    Homes, bridges, souls, the effort to turn
Unknowing tribes working alone in zeal.
Follow me so that in fevered pursuit
    With flailing sword the future strife
    And struggle might end with a single strike
To the heart of leaders with no purpose.
Our needs, longing for a sought-after sunset
    In the never-ending race to completion,
    This worthless charge pleasing crowned heads,
Heeding civilization's call to regression.
Our *homo mimeticus* can only begin
With orders refusing the slaying of men.

CHAPTER 2: IMMERSION

...then, from thee, much more must flow,
And soonest our best men with thee do go...
    —John Donne, 'Holy Sonnets 10'

YOU WILL REMAIN THE SAME YESTERDAY, TODAY, AND FOREVER

Color is not an action
To be dealt with differently
When painting with forked tongues.

Action does not trace
An untested future
Onto the wild canvas of history.

Color fills all moments,
Sketches the branch that touches
The world with familiar fingers.

Action speaks
With the force of colors
Unified through the prism of water.

Those are not white clouds.
That is not a blue sky.
We are not your red suns.

TRIBUTE TO THE SIEGE OF ORLEANS

The effect and cause, the punishment and sin,
    A form of *lectio devina*,
    Meditations as rampart to meaning,
Siege ladders lifting the heart from within,
Allowing the complete and living words
    Of well-ordered, ever-expanding nations
    To fill the gaps left by a fortress' erasure
Into moments that quell internal storms.
We soldiers though, people forever strong,
    Needs paid for in the nobleman's guilt,
    Find our footing rooted in lost youth,
In a scrambling effort to take down the wall,
Remove the evolution of this throne,
Making bodies aware of the softness of bone.

THE BAPTISM BY FIRE STARTS EARLY

The day you escape to find your calling
Will forever remain etched
In your narrative,
A story arc shared by us all:

At the bus stop a vagrant,
System's fall out,
Large sneaks unlaced,
Dirty, thrift-shop baggies,
Steals your last pack of *American Spirits*
And you will question your resolve.

The toilet at the government hotel
Is stopped up by a quickly digested
Last supper of zapped Salisbury steak,
Instant potatoes, and canned beans.
First call arrives early to deliver
A raised right hand in sacrifice.

A shuttle full of know-it-alls,
Already well acquainted,
Keep their eyes on the prize
While shifting their gaze
Between the driver
And their seat mate.

Now at the in-processing center
An administrative tool makes a joke
About leaving behind a career

As a french fry technician,
Though you have never fried potatoes,
Nor do you understand applied mechanics.

The *Sports Illustrated Swimsuit Issue*
Lying damp and flaccid in the waiting room
Feels like the last one to ever be produced,
The zenith of artistic license,
Thin exceptionalism
Peering out with disdain.

Now fly off to the training land
You saw in gray dreams,
Exotic militarized woods
Of heritage and hate,
As a new drummer leads you round
Under the strain of selfless service.

Attending your first soldier's meal
A sassy gal counts
Freshly shaved skulls
Laughing as she calls you Moby Dick,
Because of your elusiveness,
And the oil found in your junk.

Next: uniform fittings
Where the lady with the electrolarynx
Grants you one last wish
That reverberates through the halls,
Boxers or briefs?

Freeze.

You are caught in your first ambush,
Soon to be impaled by tainted punjis,
Slapped across the face
By a six pack of shit-colored boxers
With large blow holes.

On this first lonely night you will
Stumble through the domino maze
Of wool-skinned speed bumps,
Slither into the naked think-tank
To close your eyes and scrub away
The stench of your civilian past.

Low crawl into your bunk
As testimony to your commitment.
Listen:
The hero above you falls in love with porn.
The patriot to your left steals your flip-flops.
The hero to your right has killed six men already.

In another land a vagrant, without borders,
Safe and secure in his freedoms
Will smoke the last of a crushed pack
Of *American Spirits*
As you find this truth renewed in you:
Dulce et decorum est pro patria mori.

And you will one day be thanked for your service.

TO SOLDIERS' RESTITUTION
IN THE BATTLE OF SARATOGA

And thou like adamant, draw mine iron heart,
    Unable to resist, drawn as the flea
    To ill-manicured curs, the blood-tinged tea
Of loyalties poured out across two lands apart.
But efforts to rule these continents
    Must get behind me, the internal angst,
    Chased, inspected from phalanx to phalanx,
A misunderstanding of existence
For we see now there is no content.
    We are but who we are,
    Tamed by those who would see us harmed,
Blistered by the efforts of these midnight chores:
What have I become but a hardened heart,
Blinded by the need to rip our nature apart?

AN EXERCISE IN NEW IDENTITY

Go ahead.
Pick one word from column A.
And then.
Choose a word from column B.
Combine.
A new name spurs your transition:

To acceptance
To willed dissonance
To the cognitive impairment
Required of you
By those in power.
The choice is now yours.

A	B
Holy	God
Patriot	Hole
Blood	Warrior
Victim	Hood
Love	Giver
Son	Father
Little	Camper
Life	Conqueror
Myth	Taker
Barbarian	Hero
Legend	Soldier
Knight	Thought
Training	Man
Hate	Member

Whisper this new name to yourself each night
As you drift off to sleep, a meditative practice
In preparation for the callow indifference
Required to mete out violence in the name of
Retribution.

ATLAS ARRIVES

If you ever tire of having sand kicked in your face by beachside bullies, summon Atlas immediately. The world's most perfectly developed man is not a fad to be forever relegated to the back of childhood comic books. He has been waiting patiently all these years for you to call.

When you call, the titanic man of masculine fortitude will come with a solution to all your modern problems by way of muscular firepower and the threat of fisticuffs to those coastal ruffians who have ravaged the tiny space you have carved out on the shore for you and your love.

Act soon enough and the universal paradigm of strength and virility will provide you a set of x-ray specs by which you may encase the world in a thin coating of visual sleight of hand, a small dose of skeletal humor, a blurred check on the internal structures out to do you harm.

Our hero admonishes us to flex our biceps daily, curl the heart into the triumphant position, contract hidden abs in a never-ending struggle to escape the didactic commands of the bullying gentry and to walk away in search of our own unified salvation having found the dynamic tension we have sought these many years as we scraped burning sand from our frail bodies.

TO THE ILL-ADVISED CHARGE
OF ANY LIGHT BRIGADES

Is all but love, oh let this last will stand.
    The desire for action led us to watch
    As leaders create a misguided plot
To see a future in hating the land.
This is as far as foresight will allow.
    Magnificent, yes, but it is not war.
    Surely madness reigns upon the shore
Of our time, caught in the throes of a vow
To love our country wrong or right,
    Do the task or find death, no limit
    To the abuse of a peasant's plight,
Orbiting, meaningless, begging just to be… in it:
    We want you then for our army—join or die—
    So you might find grief, joy, and even more lies.

COMMUNICATION AND CORRESPONDENCE DURING SERVICE TIME

You must write to your loved ones.
Who care for you.
Who want to hear from you.
The following:

We are well, for we are tradesmen,
Skilled in the art of machinations,
Logistical support, firepower,
Identity projection, bombs.
We are warriors by proxy.

We are well prepared
For the barbarian hordes,
The fresh buffet of killing delights
Presented to us
As we ford rivers of death,
Parachute into the dark night,
Slog through the manifest
Of our sub-Saharan destiny.

We are whole.
We are one:
El Salvador del Mundo,
Who speak of a past,
As heroes and villains,
The cornucopic gods
Of all your thanksgivings.

ODE TO THE BATTLE OF SAN JUAN HILL

But, that god should be made like man, much more,
 There exists much pleasure in the divine
 Scrambling up the hill to make you mine.
This friend of the blind poet, the soldier's chore
Exacting from each other the cleaving
 Fulfillment of the romantic, ideal
 Personage, Lord and liar, bodies feel
The weight of new guns in an unholy friction.
You would do well to escape the whole
 Fight, running away from post-modern tripe.
 Release the bonds of what will be last rights
Left fluttering, languishing in Gatling guns,
 Attempting to know what sacrifice might bestow
 While remaining deaf to years of work before.

THE LIES WE TELL. TODAY AND FOREVER.

I am with you always, house training the golden goose.
I will remain with you, feather plucking the rotting carcass.

But I will only teach those with pliant hands.
I instruct only those that listen to the still small voice.

That shrill voice within that tells you:

The vets that ply me with tales of daring-do,
Are most likely to have daring-didn't.

You know the Goliath feeds off these lies, this hubris,
The breath of epics told in precious tones.
I change nothing.
So let me ask you this:

Why concern yourself with the leviathan forest,
When you have never even smelled a campfire?
So that you might feel the deep burn?
Conduct an autopsy while still drunk
On your own power to deploy?

Let's just say that now,
Now you may run ahead,
Announcing:

Such is the evolution of our stories.
Now I know that heroes are legion.
And I may cast history to a herd of pigs.

You are here to house train the golden goose.
You will remain here to feather pluck the carcass.

Experiences may vary.

AN EXPLANATION OF THE BATTLE OF GALLIPOLI

Nor ever chaste except you ravish me,
    Understanding night's journey toward our fame,
    Turning us inside out to vomit till lame,
Strain bowels till we shiver on bended knee.
I flow out of the temple veil, with luck
    Twice, then a third, to move on toward our fourth
    As the sacred heart cries for more:
More on the tip, more on the slow thrusts
That feed the hardened charge of yesterday
    Seeking to fill what was once smooth flapping
    Mendacious rendering of soft lips
To strained sips from the truth, this purest of ways.
    Through these thoughts we place our hope
    In what has become man's only way to cope.

FIRST FULL DISCUSSION ON THE MEMETICS OF SOLDIERING

A soldier arrived for duty from New York City. He claimed to be a survivor of the events of September Eleventh. Yet we now know anyone still alive after the events of September Eleventh is a survivor.

For this soldier from New York City each new day of soldierly effort—each weapon cleaned, floor buffed, vaccine taken, safety briefing heard, expended brass policed—brings him closer to those catastrophic events so that two years into his first four-year term of service to his nation he will go from just being in the city on that fateful day to touching the nosecone of the plane as it penetrates the first building.

This is how dreams are made.

By the end of his term it is so determined that this soldier's high idealism and romanticism does not fit the realities required of military service. He chokes on his own oath of allegiance, diagnosed with pre-combat disorder, sent home to defend his homeland with bumper stickers and empty threats.

These are the lofty ambitions reserved for true patriots and revolutionaries, for those who first spoke to God, and then served as interpreters during construction of the Tower of Babel.

CHAPTER 3: ACQUIESCENCE

Because I did suffer, I must suffer pain...
    —John Donne, 'Holy Sonnets 3'

WHAT WE WILL ONE DAY COMMAND

We will not soldier
In the green-hazed myopic
Chokehold of murderous hours.

We will not soldier
In the stinging haze of rain
Testing our resolve.

We will not soldier
In the summer sun
With patriot's stinging eyes.

We will not soldier
For others, the benefactors
Of our search for milk and honey.

We will soldier
In the empty futures of dead space
Found in the cross-bearer's lament.

We will soldier
In dawn's newfound light
With damp feet and rusty spear.

We will soldier
In the shadows that bring us home,
Role players in another's history.

We will soldier
In a self-interested act
Of our own respect and dignity.

WHAT WE WILL ONE DAY BE GIVEN INSTEAD

You will be called to an interview
And thanked for what you have done.

The youngest at the table will lead:
I wanted to enlist but I have bone spurs.

And you will instinctively tap your foot
To remind yourself that it's still there.

The oldest will tell you:
My father served in Korea.

And you will wonder
What does that have to do with me?

The one nearest your own age will ask:
Have you ever taught before?

And the situation becomes clear.
This job will not be yours.

You are now free to answer:
As a matter of fact… no… have you?

Because you can drop a 500-pound bomb
On a lone gunman but
They suspect you cannot control
A room full of young Catholics.

As you leave, a chorus will ring out
Thank you for your service.
To which you should always respond
Much obliged.

Because none of us did anything
They would not do
If they were not too busy sharpening rowels,
Worshipping ancestors,
And judging one's ability to drill.

WHAT WE SHOULD AGREE UPON NOW

Tell them it's the surprise that hurts most.
Stories become flatulent
When imbued with the power to inflate.

Tell them of the friends of friends
And give them the *okay… yeah*
Veteran's head nod.

Say the last thing you saw
Was the jawbone of an ass
Flying by your head.

Say you saw other trucks blown up
But yours was first.
And the trucks you later saw were split

Down the middle by letters home
And boxes of clothing,
A matador's muleta
If you ever saw one.

You can bear these *okay-yeahs*
Because we know the quiet head-nod
Gets us the disability we earned

And if we are lucky, the ten percent
Off hardware we will never deserve.

Always look left, then look right
Before dispensing with an *okay-yeah*
And that sly acknowledgement,
Before probing the ground
With a wooden stake
Looking for friendly land mines.

REQUIEM FOR THOSE GENERALLY UNDERSTOOD TO BE THE WAR POETS THAT EMERGED DURING THE TIME OF THE GREAT WAR OR, THE WAR TO END ALL WARS

This beauteous form ensures a piteous mind.
　　You may only write that which you see,
　　Only chase the past as reward for routine.
So do not think us obtuse or unkind.
This is man's harbored self, pacing the floor,
　　Announcing that *your savior has come in*,
　　Here to ensure you need never bend,
Nor ever waver while he knocks at your door.
You became a new king, the rock of our salvation,
　　Mistaking the conceit of reality
　　With the reticence in fantasy
Yet still expectant of every oblation,
　　As your work sought to mend all horror and pity,
　　Regardless of form, detached from all memory.

SOME OF THE SIMPLEST COMBAT
EXPERIENCES CAN TEACH A VALUABLE LESSON

Sometimes.
Sometimes there are no casualties.
Sometimes the enemy is an old man.

He moves his water through a garden at night, in a growing network
Of canals and mud-work dams he has been building next to this road
For years and someday he just might find himself in the wrong place.

Sometimes men should explore all possibilities.
Sometimes crops are watered at midnight.
Sometimes.

WHAT THE FATES TELL US ABOUT THE ALLIED INVASION OF NORMANDY

For us, his creatures and his foes, hath died
    A worthy death full of feigning impressions
    Cast aside for hasty transgressions
Leaving shock and awe dog-paddling in a wide
Gulf awash with letters home and red water
    Flowing from the pierced ribs of a nation
    Bobbing in bays of ancient revolution.
These our savior-souls, when men mattered,
The last soldiers in our hearts to be real.
    Shall we keep on trying to forget
    Those left behind who built the monument
That bears anonymity across the sea?
    Is this the effort to purify a soul
    Or to fill your own shallow, empty hole?

AROUND THE WORLD, UNSEEN

We are protected in livestock waste,
Sleeping softly, sweetly,
Inhaling the bitter saccharine
Smell of animal wasting.

Side by side, wet, cold, yet,
Still feigning more frigidity than necessary
In order to, with homoerotic jocularity,
Settle in:

Put your arm around me.
Get under this blanket.
Rest your head here on the shoulder
That braces the recoil of my rifle.

We are not disgusted.
We are complete, again sweet,
Living different lives
Having our own conversation
In this dreamy selfsame waste.

SYNOPSIS ON THE DEVELOPMENT OF THE WAR IN THE AIR AS UNDERSTOOD BY A POST-WAR POET

He might be weak enough to suffer woe,
    This newfound feeling, mystic air renewal
    Pursuant to manhood discovering new
Techniques to make proximity man's foe.
Jesus wept. From a distance. Setting us free.
    Bombs from his perch upon that iron cross
    Wobble and drift to that place calling us
Home to the boneyard of calvary.
For they never wept. Pilots in search of ghost clouds.
    Thoughts on their own. Selfish airborne antics
    Cling to the shape of the burning sky, manic
Heads dreaming each night of the sound
    They know death makes in the empty night,
    Now that man has run amok in distant flight.

WASH AWAY YOUR PAST
A *DEATH OF THE BALL TURRET GUNNER*
SACRIFICE FOR *FORTUNA REDUX*

From my mother's sleep I fell into the state
And stumbled into the bathroom.
Six miles from civilization, released from a dream,
I woke to the sound of animals screeching.
When I die, box me up and ship me home.

From my father's sleep I fell into the state
And struck out looking.
Six miles from home plate, tied to fields of folly,
I woke to the angelic chorus of the AC-130 gunship.
When I die, send me around the world and back again.

From my brother's sleep I fell into a state
And crouched in the bedroom.
Six miles from revolution, free from form,
I woke to the paralyzing effects of ammonia.
When I die, sing songs to me from deep in the valley.

From my neighbor's sleep I fell into a state
And ran until the fires shifted.
Six miles from victory, tethered to fear,
I woke to the buzzing electric shock of rotor blades.
When I die, pin metal wings upon my chest.

From my nation's sleep I fell into a state
And slept in Abraham's bosom.
Six miles from earth, chromium testicles froze,
I woke to endless insomnia and the nightmare heart.
When I die, tell them all I did my best.

INITIAL BRAINSTORMING SESSION
FOR THE POTSDAM DECLARATION

And death shall be no more. Death, thou shalt die
    A million tiny deaths if they will give way,
    Save a half-million suicidal hearts today.
We know how this ends. We know how they
Full stop. Caught in empire's glorious call,
    Then to arms we will go and force a tumbling,
    Relish the spiral of our new bombs fumbling
And answer the call from our trinity.
And no. For when hell unleashes her innocence,
    Neurotic thought must be cast away
    Buried in a cloud, hidden in the fray
As lost hope burns flesh with the devil's mark.
So it's agreed. They bow now, oh stubborn minds,
    To see a new world and hatred sublime.

ADVICE REGARDING YOUR FUTURE
RETIREMENT STAY AT THE HOTEL REVOLUTION

Do not book a room at The Hotel Revolution.

There is no pool or fitness center
And the free breakfast lacks certain dietary requirements.

The bumbling concierge reeks of diesel fuel,
Nitrate fertilizer, and fervor.

The gum-smacking front desk clerk will give away your reservation
To trust funders, brunch eaters, and keyboard warriors.

The room service waiters skulk in darkened hallways
Slinking along walls with Kalashnikovs they have never used.

After the dishes are done, the kitchen staff plants makeshift bombs
In the atrium that go off when no one is watching.

Better for you if you were to give up all hope
Of ever reading an honest review.

Better for you to go away quietly.
They cannot control those who refuse to patronize.

Better for you if you were to just walk away.
They have no defense for abandonment.
I just would not book a room at The Hotel Revolution,
If I were you.

TREATISE ON THE EFFICACY OF
SEARCH AND DESTROY MISSIONS

I think it mercy if thou wilt forget
    My wrongs, my indiscretions, my hopes
    Pinned to a future still too remote
To gather up within a past unmet.
I chase so I might be unchaste,
    Loosed upon all like the bright angel
    Before the fall, before providential
Glories took away love's fruitful taste.
The freedom from my loving might
    Is what I ask from this devil of hosts
    To be unburdened from this seeker's eye,
Visions haunting, moving toward what is lost.
    If we knew and might see what was in store,
    God would cede his will and give us acts of war.

YOU DESERVE A BREAK

From hiding in plain sight
As your home collapses around you.
Release this hovel
Unto mis-guided Newtonian laws
Dividing you from the earth.

From the anxious sleep
That gives you a twisted face.
Release these night fears
So that Copernicus
No longer lords over your soul.

From the sound a single termite makes
When faced with petrified adversity.
Release the constant buzz
Of Cartesian thinking,
Which causes your vibrational panic.

From brunch.
From feeds.
From gluten-free bread.
From sports.
From the extreme wings
Of your vinyasa
And the taste of sweat on your lip.
From maps, compasses,
And pace counts.
From this conceit.

So that you may believe in your heart,
—Born of Augustus,
Broken by Justinian,
Held aloft by Charlemagne—
That the rumbling in your gut is hope.

From their reality
Now understood as a mirage.
Release the ancients
Unto the dustbin of history
So that you may start this journey anew.

A SACRED RITE OF PENANCE
FOR NEW COMBAT VETERANS

We do hereby confess that we have lost every war.

We relinquished our red badges behind a mud-wall during an ambush
because someone else was supposed to be in charge
and it would only add more chaos to the situation
if we leapt up with only three months left
till we went home and began directing
those looking to us for guidance
so we gave a look that said
it will be over soon,
this isn't your fight,
just sit tight.

We hunkered down, found cover, and watched as the injured hobbled
in a hail of bullets to be patched up just to run in again
to their own idea of safety and hope
as the buzzing helicopters flew by
and future lawyers writers
abusers sandwich artists
suicides preachers
and generals
fought
on.

So weeks and months and years of misunderstood orders directives
adjudications new wine in old casks served as a service guide
a *we did our part* instruction manual of the perplexed
in wave after wave of foul misguided offenses
we marked time to a more examined assault
on the senses approaching warfare
with the learned understanding
of what each bullet portends
whizz: damn time to move
zing: whoah, get down.

Now the others say
move to the next village
or *your lies will catch up to you*
as they implore you with their hearts
and we are sorry because men should kill
each other face to face as if what the lion does
not know could ever hurt him for what the others fear
is the contrition of soldiers behind mud-walls and a failure to heed
instructions they knew were wrong and they fear what will happen
if we ever just stood up to face the hail of bullets that *whizz* and *zing*
    by our heads.

A LESSON IN MILITARY VALUES: LOYALTY, DUTY, HONOR, RESPECT, SELFLESS SERVICE, PERSONAL COURAGE

Our integrity seeks out loyalty,
A juried embarkation of duty
And commitment abroad out of respect
To those unaware of selfless service.
    Viewed from a distance, placating honor,
    Time and space cede to personal courage.

And found inside this personal courage
Lies the integrity nestled in loyalty.
Like a thief devoid of a man's honor,
Crippling him in his stalwart duty
    To unseat the sought-after selfless service.
    He will soon die, lacking all respect.

The others do not see the shallowest respect
We take for granted. Our moral courage
Hides inside this selfless service, integrity
Mistaken for loyalty. It is our
    Solemn duty to never be seen then,
    Masquerading in honors as if real.

Honor becomes the patsy, the red herring
That fails to respect our commitment.
Empty duty lacking purpose,
Our physical courage girds integrity
    To the point of creating loyalties
    Ineffectual in service to self.

How then to selflessly serve?
What is more honorable than death?
What more loyal than life?
Others pay lip service to respect
    As if integral to avoiding cowardice.
    Asking what is our duty to our fellow man?

I will tell you your obligation is not
To the ego. Anything less is a disservice.
You may be brave, but internalized
Glory alludes us as it must,
    Ever courteous to this higher calling
    Of commitment pumping your bleeding heart.

To the selfless service you most respect,
    Personal courage fails to honor,
        Fails to uphold the integrity found
        In the light of our conscience.

CHAPTER 4: TRANSCENDENCE

As humorous is my contrition
As my profane love, and as soon forgot...
   —John Donne, 'Holy Sonnets 19'

TO PROMISES OF A COLD WAR

As if thou had'st seal'd thy pardon with thy blood,
    Sacrifices not asked for, effort wasted.
    Yet there, just the same, the dual-masted
X upon which to bear our love.
Playing advocate, devil's fervor,
    Airing dirty laundry on a line,
    Waving soiled white linens
At time as if this might be threatening.
Disengage and forget what was done.
    Do not allow us to tear down your altar,
    But rather, let us build another,
A shrine to all that we have become,
    A testament to our beauty, our wit,
    A monument to all modern bullshit.

WAKE UP, OH MEN OF ACTION

Men used to hide their disorders down deep,
Ashamed, a by-product of invasion.
Men took their anger out on the lawnmower,
The wife, the kids, the television set,
Squat jobs attended to in crisp, white shirts,
Punching the putrid green time clock in hopes
You might make your way home, once again.

Returning from distant wars, men stop
Midway to be greeted by angelic Europeans,
A by-product of invasion. Disembarking
They buy a massage for twenty hard-earned dollars.
Conquered hands work through the disorder,
Hiding in recesses of distant schools
Where no child can ever be left behind.

Men used to wear natty suits every day,
Tip hats to the ladies for whom they fought,
Open doors for those too timid to push back.
But to never leave a fallen comrade
Means different things to indifferent men,
Men who find it increasingly difficult to fight
With a copy of *Paradise Lost* tucked under their arm.

FIRST EXPOSURE TO THE PROS AND CONS OF A CULT OF PERSONALITY AS VIEWED IN HINDSIGHT

He was not your typical leader.

But you will recall him as the officer with the longest sideburns in the brigade, the officer that didn't like to blouse his boots on patrol, the officer whose assault pack just had to be a little different than everyone else.

You will remember him as the leader who believed putting camouflage paint on your face before a mission was as important as having a good plan, the psychological make-up of the warrior going to work. You will recall his chin strap dangling free of the three days growth he showcased while out on patrol as testament to his masculinity.

If you remember correctly, he was the one officer who strode through enemy villages with a cigarette extender, a long flowing scarf, and an air of superiority that you thought the command found threatening.

You can assume then, based on your memories, that he never allowed himself to be judged by his loyalty to higher, but rather, by his loyalty to his inner self, his emboldened character, his ability to kill at will, his plans as elaborate as his perfectly coiffured combat hair, checked in the sunny glint of his vintage compass, a complement to his Italian-made Combat boots.

And so we will now collectively recall that George Armstrong Custer may have met his match at Little Big Horn but we can rest easy knowing he was at least allowed the dignity and personal vanity provided by his shaggy locks, a wide brimmed hat perfectly askance, and the blood red scarf that flowed down into his frontier shirt and provided a sense of comfort each time he turned and twisted in the saddle to fire his guns at an enemy who refused to genuflect to his eccentricities.

YOU WILL MISS MANY LESSONS
WHILE BEING DRAGGED ACROSS THE GLOBE
SUCKLING ON THE DEFLATED TEAT OF DESTINY

With tired, aching feet,
Sleep soundly, securely,
Knowing the gods protect,
Forever proud of our work
In the name of love and hate,
Prickishness and miscalculation.

We fought as the best
Of our generation raced to retire,
Ran to the temples of youth,
Lifted arms to the chapel goddess
While the immortal hippie
Sang *Hare Krishna*.

Those aging prophets,
All natural haired and sandaled,
Led us headlong into the woods
To choke out errant thoughts
While their tiny crowns stretched forth
From bushy brambles.

Elders practiced the laying on of hands
Casting out demons of oppression,
Of idolatry, of lust, of terror,
To rid us of the desire
To drink chai with our enemies,
Rather than lager with our peers.

Disciples professed us as kings
While obscuring the emptiness
Found in crooks and crannies, all part
Of the laughter coming from their mouth,
As we pierced the crease of laugh lines
Etched in their globe-like skin.

Their pandering, laughing at bad jokes,
Going down familiar roads,
Perfecting the habit of sucking
The life out of a day's hard work,
Keeps us pleased, swallowed whole
By our fulfilled destiny.

These side-eyes of new idolators stay wide
To disorder and chaos, the devil may care
Swashbuckling, sword rattling
That calls for the death of our gods
At the hands of consumption
In a Dickens novel.

The high priest screams *it is finished*
While asking us to rewrite temple history
So that every battle
—an improvement on the last,
Every prophet
—a new teat to suckle.

NOW I PRESUME THERE WILL BE AN AFTERMATH TO THE GLOBAL WAR ON TERROR WHEREIN THIS MUST BE WHERE WE GET OFF

For thus I leave the world, the flesh, and devil
Saying: *Get behind me, relieve my angst.*
Cradle each thought, bereft of this stance.
I guess we just liked the feel of it all.

Damn it to hell then this moment of need,
Post life. Post real. Newly stale and listless,
Memories but a faint shrinking shred
Of names that sought false liberty.

So nail me to St. Andrew's cross,
In the fashion of mythic martyrs
To shake out my truth with the survivors
Who spend their lives of desperation
Trying to forget the alpha, omega,
God's spitting on the lips of Cassandra.

IN HAND-TO-HAND BATTLES, YOU MUST CLOSE THE DISTANCE

You are no longer a work in progress but rather a new creature
  of hope
Lived in moments when your orders were to never question why.

Release civilized hands to free float towards a future
Outlined in waypoints mapped in the sky
Set along escape routes laid out over millennia
Handed down through generations.

A quick, centering look around the room should soothe
The head
Remind you that you no longer need to punch

As Germanicus punched Little Boot
As Alexander punched Hephaestion

For the berserker in you punched and fought past tense.

So when the sensible business slacks at the public park gets angry
at the love in your heart, you will have already proven your metal.
When the high-lifted patriot cuts you off or the keyboard warrior
with purple-hearted gamer thumbs questions your virility, you will
have already punched hard, punched often.

You need no longer worry, no longer wonder if you have the
minerals. No need to fret over how you might sleep at the end of the
day because you are yourself the punch-loving hoplite. And you may
now ignore all the laws of land warfare.

UPON SEEING PATRIOTIC FERVOR
IN FUTURE WARS

That being red, it dyes red souls to white,
    Dogmatic florilegium formed
    At muzzle tip to enclose my
Enemies in the fragrance sought in lover's

Respite.

But truth might yet be found in a dying spirit's glow,
    Escaping the howl of a boomer
    Generation still running a monte.

Exposed.

Blue hearts, revealed soul, lost.

Seeking

A renaissance of conquest. Were we that blind:

To the newly styled *hey, war is swell*?
To the golden road leading straight to… well?

Or deep down we knew our station in life
Would easily fall at first signs of strife.

So I cannot shake what remains inside,
Only seek to hide in a world no longer mine.

ABSTRACT THOUGHT MUST STILL CONTAIN ELEMENTS OF THE CONCRETE

The day begins.
Dense fog waltzes in evenly spaced gaps.
Sun's morning rays introduce new characters,
A casual reminder that possession
Of arms, legs, a spleen, the beating heart,
Coalesce to the movement of time.

Feel blank.
Velvet masquerading as fur after taxidermy.
The rudiments of the unknowable,
Stretching the hypotenuse,
Connecting the opposite,
Creating a tribal formation.

Eavesdrop on Wagner.
Hiding in the darkest of mines.
Wait for the triumph of lengthening discord.
Music blossoming,
Into that fogged head,
Launching into suspicions.

Act of ablutions found in the stripping
Of liner notes buried in Teutonic myth,
Basking in audible light,
Seeking the last man
Drowned on the *Titanic*
You always believed to be on your left.

—Besides, the last words
   of the crew
   on that sinking
Behemoth, temple
   to human potential,
      might have been…
okay guys, pump the brakes

      as they were condemned
         to the deep
             primordial
       darkness

Co-sign free hearts and liberated minds
To the cause. Let the taste of victory
Carry us away on the back
Of a single Valkyrie, relief
From the duty of turning big rocks
Into ever smaller rocks for the masses.

Aggressions weaken in time,
An opportunity to softly stroke
The apex of the triumvirate,
Brotherhood of completeness,
Until the line no longer holds,
The center shattered by lack of interest.

Abandonment signals the end
Of a thousand-year reign
Dragged along by enlarged memories
Engorged generalities, fertile deltas

Waiting to impregnate future gardens
Shared with an empty earth.

The day ends, as all others,
A wasteland of beating hearts,
Spleens, arms, and legs, marching,
Coalescing to seal the gaps
On which we first laid violent eyes
Toward killing the dawn's early light.

ON KILLING

And Satan hates me, yet is loath to lose me,

This line intentionally left blank.

His countenance glistening in my own sweat,

This lite intentionally left blank.

The beautiful one fully attuned

This life intentionally left blank.

To the light which shines within all men,

This life intentionally left flank.

Wresting hope from those who know not what they do

This lie intentionally left blank.

While dripping sweat into the eyes of Argos

This lie intentionally left.

So that memories are erased, cast away,
Via shifting hearts as our heroes sway.

MANAGING EXPECTATIONS

When Jesus returns, let's hope he is riding a state-of-the-art jetpack.
Let us pray that the Son of Man levitates to his terrestrial domain
like a tycoon with an exploratory toy to take up those fortunate
souls who have chosen to follow Him during their sojourn with
the Philistines. Let us hope and pray the Messiah sweeps us to glory
towards the golden path of progress and the loving spread of the
news that we have all waited for, the news that will make our enemies
weep.

Let us hope he is smiling.
Let us all pray he is the short-haired, toothy, gentile Jesus we know
    and cherish.
Let us hope the Son of the Most-High God says:

Come unto me.
I am the light of the world.
Ask and it will be given.

Maybe he will bring wine.
Perhaps he will bring a cheese platter.

What none of us want is the long-haired, leather-faced, crows-feet
Jesus who flips over tables in the temple marketplace, says *turn the
other cheek*, and has spent the last 2000 years making sure we see his
ripped abs above every altar in Christendom.

What we want is a messiah for the world we have made, a savior who will swoop down like the breezy-haired, linen-clothed, billionaire guru, silicone mold, in perfect control, on a mission, with a purpose, a messiah who will look us each directly in the eye and say:

Well done my good and faithful servant.
Thank you for your power.
Thank you for your truth.
How about a ride on my jetpack?

When the Redeemer returns, let us pray for pure hearts, clear minds, and a full rack of armor-piercing nails.

WE CAN STILL WIN THIS THING YOU KNOW

If you let us,
    If you will listen,
If you have learned anything
    About insurgencies,
About psychology,
    About how to fight,
About migrations,
    About the hypotenuse,
About life,
    About taxidermy,
About sleep cycles,
    About marksmanship,
About philosophy,
    About flanking,
About charging,
    About patience,
About the life
    That burns within,
About stand-off,
    About mil-dots,
About logistics,
    About purity,
About hope,
    And kindness,
About the light
    You see inside us all,
And the way a mountain moves
Of its own accord when the feet of fighters
Scramble up and down rock-strewn ribs

Making plans to unload burdens
At the peak just beyond the horizon.

UPON WAKING IN THE MIDDLE OF THE NIGHT

It is always oh-dark-thirty
When the pitching, rolling out of bed,
Shuffling into dim spaces
To dream of revolutions
While inspecting dreams firsthand
That distract from true desire.

Over there lie fallen poppy petals, worn from blossoming,
Auburn fields, cracked and dry from overuse.

Over there lies an eager unknown geography, the raging
Riverbed to come for the battlefield, the sweetest of cries.

Over there keeps us compliant in the chase, the hope
Of a sprinkling action, hardened memories,
Another triumph in the act of self-destructive emissions.

THOUGHTS ON THE FUTURE OF CIVILIZATION WHILE SITTING IN THE DOCTOR'S EXAMINING ROOM WAITING FOR MY ANNUAL EXAM

Men will sit on the toilet
Rather than stand to piss
Preferring quick flicks of their twitter
To holding their personality in tiny hands.

The prophet will open
A wide-open gap in your neighborhood.
The son will no longer live in your heart
Preferring the comfort provided by a basement futon.

A neutered patriarchy dies of boredom
As princesses, tickled pink by their trim
Electric Volvos, vibrate down slick roads,
While the Nerf-man riding shotgun watches.

Adult males will dress like they're twelve,
Copulate as if sixteen:
Lost and fumbling, fast and self-involved,
As if they never knew their mother could be so hot.

Surviving offspring will fail to understand
The Pythagorean Theorem as nothing more
Than instructions for love, a proof
For creating space within safety-colored playgrounds.

Humynkind will continue to exterminate the alien,
The slowest rhinos, the stupidest dolphins, and the oak
That once held a community together
Will rot and die exclaiming *nothing is forever*.

And you—there—clinging to the sad height,
Stand ever fast,
Gaze straight into my eyes and say
That mole on your back has always looked the same.

TOOLS FOR THE DUFFEL BAG YOU WILL CARRY WHEN YOU FINALLY FIND PARADISE

Take note of the neighbors on their deck,
Boom-boom-booming their celebrations,
Enfilade to your darkest dreams.

Stand guard, look round, in a watchful crouch
As someone cuts their grass on our Lord's day
A scant two hundred yards away.

In this whirling haze of memories
High-crawl to the toolshed,
Twenty-five hard yards away, seeking cover.

Center your bubbles.
Center down.
Have salt in yourself my friends.

Consider your only options
To be the pulling of your own molars
Or to wallow in the mechanical pain of now.

Choose wisely and grip with both hands
The rusty pliers that will see to the demise
Of a once-pristine, tribal mouth.

The twisting, turning of a bear claw grip
In your bloody maw, the succulent taste of copper
Coats a throat eager for payment.

Drift into the dull roar of the echo chamber,
The blur thickening—soothing, unfocused—
Leave this cacophony of the takers.

Begin your three-to-five-second rush
Out of the tool shed, button hook
To behold your new actions.

A new skillset for the old
Kit bag, drugged as ever
For the common man,

These cues for action evolve in us,
Piercing like the eyes of one
Who gave sight to the blind.

Yet evil blames a naive failure
To see the hope offered in exchange
for a flogging in ancient streets.

We know the cries of a desperate nation
Are a revolution's most passionate,
Throes of desire swelling in the tiniest of slights.

A wide controlling web built on the freedom
Of you at the expense of all others
Is a symptom of madness.

I am you and you are me and our land
Will again be a playground for hide and seek,
A gathering garden of new vines on old trunks,

Our own saga of mythic memories
Stand guard, look round, in a watchful crouch.
Wear this sword until you can no more,

And count the steps toward your reformation.
For we now have a past and it is ours to seize,
Onward, toward His kingdom found within,
These new battle drills for the modern warrior.

NOTES AND ACKNOWLEDGEMENTS

Nineteen poems utilize the last line of one of John Donne's
Holy Sonnets as the first line of a new work.

The author would like to thank the following journals for their
support in publishing several of the individual pieces contained
in this manuscript:

—*Tahoma Literary Review* for 'The Transformation We Must
Endure' as 'The Cocoon'

—*F(r)iction* for 'Around the World, Unseen' (reprinted with
permission from *Oh Dark Thirty*)

—*Bridge Eight Literary Journal* for 'You Will Remain the Same
Yesterday, Today, and Forever' as 'Word to Your Mother'

—*Oh Dark Thirty* for 'The Breakfast of Superstars' as 'The Breakfast
of a Tiny Empire', 'Advice Regarding Your Future Retirement Stay
at Hotel Revolution' as 'Hotel Kabul: a Review', and 'One Item on
a To-Do List We Are Guaranteed to Never Complete' as 'An Item
on a To-Do List Never To Be Completed'

And finally, many thanks to the incredible BSPG/Eyewear Publishing
Team for their support; especially Amira, Cate, and Todd.